My Civic Adventure: Learning about Voting and Community!

A Fun Guide to Learning About Civics and Voting

Written by Alisa L. Grace

Illustrations by naqsa_art

This Book is Dedicated to:

To our future voters, we desire that children learn about civics and the voting process in a fun and engaging manner. We are committed to engaging them in learning about civics and the vital role of all parties involved in ensuring the success of our voting process.

Dear Parents and Teachers,

We are excited to share "My Civic Adventure: Learning About Voting and Community!" This delightful and educational resource is designed for children aged 3-5. It's an excellent way to introduce our youngest learners to the important concepts of civics and voting in a fun and engaging manner.

Why is this book important for 3-5 year-olds?

1. Early Civic Engagement: Introducing children to civics early on helps them understand their community and their role within it. Learning about how our community and government work and the importance of voting fosters a sense of belonging and responsibility.

2. Simple and Fun Learning: The book uses age-appropriate language and colorful illustrations, making complex ideas accessible and enjoyable. Through these vibrant pictures, children can grasp essential concepts while having fun.

3. Foundation for Future Learning: Early exposure to civics concepts lays the groundwork for more complex understanding as children grow. It encourages curiosity and a desire to participate in community activities, setting the stage for lifelong civic engagement.

4. Encouraging Family Discussions: This book is a fantastic resource for sparking meaningful conversations at home and in the classroom. It allows parents and teachers to discuss the importance of voting and being active in the community with young children.

5. Building Good Habits: Learning about civics and voting helps children develop good habits like thinking about others, following rules, and making informed decisions. These skills are invaluable and will benefit them throughout their lives.

We hope that "My Civic Adventure: Learning About Voting and Community!" will be valuable to your educational resources, inspiring our youngest generation to become informed and engaged citizens. Thank you for supporting early civic awareness and participation.

Warm regards,

Alisa L. Grace

"Welcome to Our Civic Adventure!"
Hey kids! Today, we're going to talk about something called civics. Civics is all about learning how our community and government work. Imagine our community is like a big team, and everyone has a role to play. One very important civics activity is voting. Voting is like making a choice together. It helps us decide what we want to do as a big team. So, when we vote, we all have a say in making decisions that benefit our community. Isn't that cool?

"CIVICS = COMMUNITY + VOTING."

The Supervisor of Elections

"Meet the Supervisor of Elections"

This person has a significant job. They help organize and oversee elections to make sure everything runs smoothly. They ensure everyone can vote quickly and that all the votes are counted correctly. It's like they're the coach of our extensive team, helping us make choices together. Isn't that great?

Supervisor of Elections

Register & Vote

"What is Civics?"

Civics is about learning how our community works. It means understanding the rules we follow and how we help make decisions. Voting is a meaningful way we do this. Everyone gets to choose what they think is best for the community. It's fun, isn't it?

"Registering to Vote"

To be able to vote, people need to sign up first. This is called voter registration. It's important because it helps make sure everyone who wants to vote is ready to do it. When people sign up to vote, they get to help make decisions that are good for our community. Registration gives everyone a chance to choose what they think is best. Isn't that neat?

REGISTRATION
BOOTH

"Helpers on Election Day"

On voting day, there are special helpers called poll workers. Poll workers have important jobs. They help people sign in, give out the right ballots to vote, and ensure everyone knows what to do. They also help keep everything running smoothly. Poll workers are important because they ensure voting is easy and fair. Isn't that great?

"The Voting Tools"

On election day, we use special machines and tools to help us vote. There are voting machines where people press buttons or touch screens to choose what they want. There are also paper ballots where people can mark their choices with a pen. These tools help count all the votes quickly and correctly. The voting tools make sure everyone's vote is heard. Isn't that cool?

VOTE

BALLOT BOX

"Spreading the Word"

The Outreach Department has a special job. It helps teach people about voting and why it's important. It tells everyone when and where to vote and helps them understand how to do it. The Outreach Department ensures everyone knows their vote matters and encourages them to join in and make choices for our community. Isn't that wonderful?

VOTE YOUR OWN

VOTE YOUR OWN

YOUR VOTE IS YOUR VOICE

7

"How Do We Vote?"

Let's learn how we vote! Here's what happens on election day:

Arrive at the Polling Place: First, we go to a special place called the polling place. This is where people vote.

POLLING STATION

POLL WORKER

Sign-In: When we get there, we tell the helpers our name. They check a list to find our name and make sure we are ready to vote.

Get a Ballot or Use a Machine: Next, the helpers give us a paper called a ballot or guide us to a voting machine. These are what we use to make our choices.

Make Choices: We mark our choices on the ballot with a pen or touch the screen on the voting machine to pick what we think is best.

Submit the Vote: After we make our choices, we put the ballot in a special machine to count the votes.And that's it! Our vote is counted, and we help make decisions for our community. Isn't that fun?

"And the Winner Is..."

After everyone votes, it's time to count the votes. Once all the votes are counted, we determine who got the most votes. The person with the most votes is the winner. This is how we make decisions together. Isn't that exciting?

10

"Your Vote, Your Voice"

Voting is very important because it helps our community. When we vote, we help make choices about things like parks, schools, and leaders. Everyone's vote is like their special voice saying what they think is best. When everyone votes, it makes our community a better place for everyone. Isn't that amazing?

11

"Be a Civic Hero!"

You can be a civic hero by talking to your family about voting. Ask them about elections and why voting is important. As a child, you can be excited to participate in elections one day and help make choices for your community. Being a civic hero means using your voice to improve things for everyone. Isn't that wonderful?

Civic Hero

"Words to Know"

Hello, future voters! Here are some important words to know:

Community: The place where we live, play, and work together.

Government: A group of people who help make rules and keep our community running smoothly.

Civics: Learning about how our community and government work.

Voting: Making choices together to decide what is best for our community.

Voter Registration: Sign up to be able to vote.

Poll Workers: Special helpers who ensure voting goes smoothly on Election Day.

Ballot: A piece of paper where we mark our choices when we vote.

Voting Machine: A special machine we use to make and count our votes.

Outreach Department: A group of people who teach others about voting and encourage them to participate.

Election: A special time when we vote to make decisions for our community.

"Thanks for Learning with Us!"

Thank you for learning about voting and our community with us. Voting is very important because it helps us make good choices together. When you grow up, you can use your vote to help make our community a happy and fun place for everyone. Isn't that wonderful? Thanks for being such great learners!

DEMOCRACY

vote for USA

The Supervisor of Elections

15

I VOTED TODAY

VOTE

Election Day

24

VOTE

WHY VOTING MATTERS

decisions	voice
community	future

1) Empowering connections for a vibrant

   _____

2) _____ shape our path forward

3) Building a brighter _____ together

4) Your _____ matters

(Answers 1. community, 2. decisions, 3. future, 4. voice)

9) What is the unique list where all the registered voters' names are kept?

10) What do we call the process of counting votes?

Answers 1. Election, 2. Democracy, 3. The Supervisor of Elections, 4. Ballot, 5. Poll Worker, 6. Photo and Signature ID, 7. Scanner, 8. Accuracy, 9. Voter Registration Database, 10. Tabulation

ASSISTING VOTERS

Meet the Author

Meet Alisa Ladawn Grace, a retired school administrator, Chief Operating Officer of a nonprofit company, Transformation Life Coach, and a fervent advocate for children's civic education. Alisa has authored not one but three engaging and informative children's books focused on civics: "Civic Heroes: Discovering Elections with the Supervisor of Elections" (ages 6-9), "My Civic Adventure: Learning About Voting and Community!" (ages 3-5), and "Election Essentials with the Supervisor of Elections: A Guide to Civics for Young Citizens" (ages 10-13).

Recognizing the importance of early civic education, Alisa's books introduce children to fundamental concepts like democracy, voting rights, and the electoral process in an age-appropriate and enjoyable way. Her work aims to inspire the next generation of informed and responsible voters, empowering them to participate in their communities and actively shape a better future.

Alisa's belief in the potential of young minds is deeply rooted in her diverse experiences. From her career in education to her role as a Transformation Life Coach, she has seen firsthand the transformative power of guidance. Her passion for guiding individuals toward personal growth and spiritual fulfillment is a belief and a mission evident in her writing.

Alisa's practical guide, "Unlocking Your Great Potential Within You: The Supernatural Powers of Meditation, Executive Functioning Skills, and Good Habits for Kids 3-18 Years Old," Is not just a book but a toolkit for success and well-being. It equips children with tools they can apply immediately, emphasizing the importance of faith, integrity, and love in an immediately applicable way.

Through her writing, Alisa seeks to make a positive difference in the lives of children and families, fostering a lifelong commitment to civic engagement and unlocking the great potential of every young citizen.

www.ingramcontent.com/pod-product-compliance
Lightning Source LLC
LaVergne TN
LVHW061331060426
835513LV00015B/1357